oh, goodness

the Bible study

oh, goodness
the Bible study

Discovering God's goodness for ourselves.

Maria Hatch-Bowersock

Unless otherwise noted, all Scripture is from:

Scriptures marked NIV are taken from the NEW INTERNATIONAL VERSION (NIV): Scripture taken from THE HOLY BIBLE, NEW INTERNATIONAL VERSION ®. Copyright© 1973, 1978, 1984, 2011 by Biblica, Inc.TM. Used by permission of Zondervan

Scriptures marked ESV are taken from the THE HOLY BIBLE, ENGLISH STANDARD VERSION (ESV): Scriptures taken from THE HOLY BIBLE, ENGLISH STANDARD

This Bible study is dedicated to my dear Named Free Ministries team. Your service will forever be etched in my memory as remembrance stones (Joshua 4).

Contents

Week Three

Week Four

Week Five

From the Author

This Bible study was written as a follow up to my book, "oh, goodness". The book was written with the purpose of getting you curious about discovering God's goodness in your own life. This Bible study, however, is written with the purpose of equipping you to tell of it after you discover it. How awesome would it be if every one of you wrote your own story of God's goodness?

I am not ashamed to say that my prayer continues to be that we won't just know but have faith that God is good. I spent seven years writhing in grief, pain, loss, and anxiety all stemming from this question, "How can this be good?!" I heard people try to encourage me with words, trying to convince me terrible tragedy was a part of God's plan and therefore good. I was confused, alone, and felt hopeless. It was in that place God began to teach me, through his word, about his goodness. What I found was something different than what others had tried to describe. I am sharing my journey with you because I believe sharing is what God calls us to do. We are going to read his word, meditate on his word, and consider his word through this study.

The discovering of one's story often requires a journey back to remember and reflect, and the study is set up that way- as a journey. You will notice I use language that suggests we are on an actual journey because I don't want you to miss that our relationship with Jesus is more like a journey than a formula.

I am praying for you as you prepare to take a journey that will set you free in Christ: discovering God's goodness when life isn't good.

to your freedom,
Maria Hatch - Bowersock
p.s. If you are to share your story, please do so at www.namedfreeministries.com

What to Expect

I would like to provide you with some helpful tips before you embark on this journey. Below, I've listed some of those tips in bullet points.

Tips :

- Anything in **bold** is an assignment to complete or an important message I don't want you to miss.
- "Truth for Your Soul" is your nourishment for the journey that day; you'll want to mediate on that specific scripture the entire day.
- "Today's Focus" is your focus for that day's assignment and Scripture to come back to as you journey through the day.
- Throughout this journey I will be using the English Standard Version and New International Version of the Bible.
- I share some of my personal journal entries for women who learn through stories. If you do not find these helpful, please consider disregarding them.

Oh, Goodness the Bible Study

Week One

Reflecting on God's Love for You

Day 1

Meet the Friend

*

Today's Focus: *Having loved his own who were in the world, he loved them to the end.* (John 13:1b ESV)

Reflections from a Former Fear Monger
My parents were killed in a plane crash on June 24, 2011, and it stained my life forever. When my parents died, I experienced unrestrained and unreserved grief. After that experience, I knew I never, ever, wanted to feel pain like that again. In fact, if you were sitting across from me right now, you'd hear the emphasis on "ever" and my broken voice, with tears welling in my eyes. I had known pain before but never to that degree.

Unwelcome change comes to all of us at some point, in some form. Life is fleeting. Christian or not, we can all agree on the fact that we aren't doing this thing forever. So, as you can imagine, I have been in this constant state of tug-o-war with God. Only, he's not playing. My pride tells me he is and that I can somehow "out tug" him to be in control. It wasn't until recently that I finally dropped the rope and stopped playing. I surrendered. I continue surrendering because he keeps being worth it, and because he has provided me with such a lightness and rest in the undoing of my control. This, Dear One, is what a person experiencing true joy feels.

I've always wondered what it was like to experience joy in its truest form. It's like I had been living as Miss Havisham did in the novel Great Expectations: *spending a long life away from sunlight only to finally realize the sun is just beyond the door!*

The change has come slowly, but as I move closer to freedom, I'm seeing more of him and more of me. He has revealed pieces of himself, which in turn reveals my true heart condition. One of the things the Lord is teaching me is that my fear is keeping me from experiencing and giving true love (and I'm not referring to the "cheesed up" version either). True love takes vulnerability, knowing there will be pain and grief amid the joy and beauty. Love is going to hurt if I love like Jesus loved because it's vulnerable, the only real way to love.

"Love." This word is plastered all over social media, bumper stickers on the car driving in front of us, and all throughout the shows we watch to unwind in the evening. Not only is it everywhere, but these avenues are defining love for us by telling us what it is, how it looks, and what we do to receive love. The world has defined love for us (even down to the emoji hearts) but so has God through his word. Both definitions are not created equal, making it vital for us to know the real thing over imitation.

For that very reason, as a starting place for today, let's define true love by looking at 1 Corinthians 13. **Please record how God's Word defines love by looking at verses 4 – 7.**

Let's allow this biblical description of love to soak in and let it permeate your mind. In doing so, let's take this one step further by comparing this to how the world may define love. **In the space provided below, list possible differences between the world's definition and God's definition of love.**

> *If you are struggling with a part of God's definition of love, tell him! Relationships are hard and understanding God's love is met with challenges. So, tell him these parts of you and ask him for eyes to see and a heart to hear before you decide to begrudge him.*

<u>World's Definition</u>   <u>God's Definition</u>

Keep all this information stored up in your mind as we head over to meet with Judas and Jesus. There is so much to experience in John 13, but for our purposes in the next few days, our main characters are going to be Judas and Jesus.

Let's start getting some good traction by reading John 13:1 – 17.

> **Please, please don't gloss over this part because it's the meat of what we are doing here in this study. It would be like skimming a book and saying you know what it's about when really, you are missing out on experiencing the full picture. Let's not be skimmers of God's Word!*

For memory sake, write verse 2 below.

Jesus, about to be betrayed by Judas — his friend, his follower, one of his "persons" — washed Judas' feet knowing his "friend" was about to betray him in the worst way. A way that a friendship just doesn't come back from. It is in our closest relationships we often feel the most pain, isn't it? **How does this specific act of love Jesus showed for Judas impact you? Record your thoughts below.**

I don't know about you, but these verses cause me to pause. My mind couldn't help but travel back to this day in John 13 and wonder what Jesus was feeling during this encounter with Judas. I can't help but wonder what desires or longings he may have had knowing his friend would betray him. I'm also struck by Judas' ability to go through with the betrayal, especially with the amount of history their friendship had. Regardless, the fact remains that in spite of Judas' betrayal, Jesus washed his feet with the rest of the disciples he loved.

Take time to write out the second half of verse 1 below, starting with "He had loved…"

Jesus had loved his disciples until the very end, even his betrayer. Now, let's take this truth and merge it with 1 Corinthians 13. I love merging Scripture because it gives such a rich picture of truth!

Below, record how Jesus showed love to Judas on this day the disciple became the betrayer.

It can be easy to read this Scripture at a distance, but, truth be told, we are the women on these pages of Scripture. So, we end our first day together by welcoming the Holy Spirit to prune out of us what is dead, separating us from our Savior. For us, this starts with the revealing of Jesus' love toward us through the lives of two men: Judas and Peter. Welcome to this grand narrative of Scripture. I am so honored to embark on this journey with you.

As we close today, take some time to ponder what impacts you about this scene in John 13.

Day 2

Jesus Loves the Betrayer & Denier

*

Today's Focus: *Now before the Feast of the Passover, when Jesus knew that his hour had come to depart out of this world to the Father, having loved his own who were in the world, he loved them to the end.* (John 13:1 ESV)

Reflections from a Former Fear Monger [part 2]
a year before my parents died in a plane crash
I could be sitting among the beauty of nature with the sun shining, green surrounding me, the smell of fresh flowers permeating as if it were my perfume, and yet feel so dead inside. Any part of me that was once carefree was now gone, and all that was left was a deep sadness, shame, and guilt which was suffocating me, taking the air right out from my lungs.

I remember one day in particular. I was sitting on my parents' back porch, in one of my mom's nicely cushioned patio chairs. As I was looking out over the golf course, I began to think about how good my life was and how I should be enjoying life, but I wasn't because of this shame that stuck to me like a leech. The thought I had next will be one that is forever remembered in my mind because it became the day I realized the reality of how far from God I had traveled, "I'm going to die here as a slave to my bondage." Have you heard of the television show called, The Walking Dead? *Well, that would be a perfect description of what it was like to be me or to be around me — I was the walking dead. All joking aside, my soul was dying and there was nothing funny about that to me.*

I had become a person I never knew could exist inside of me. I was twenty-four and publicly wearing the shame and guilt of being a young, Christian divorcee. I then spent months post-divorce really solidifying my shame through tragic choices I made. I had the logic of an idiot at the time; my thinking went something like this, "Well, I already blew it, so I might as well run myself off a cliff and really blow it."

I became that woman I once judged, and I was so ashamed. At one time, I was arrogant enough to think I was "better than" the type of women who gave their bodies away. Little did I realize that arrogance was ignorance. Yet, there I was, sitting in the filth of doing the very things I said I would never do. I thought my life was over. Judgement sounds from the Enemy rang loud, and I began to believe I was worthless, unforgiven, and all out of do-overs. Little did I know I was about to come face-to-face with my Savior, and I would never be the same again.

There is one glaring difference between me and Judas, and it is one that makes all the difference as far as salvation is concerned: Judas may have felt guilt over his sin, but it was never met with repentance. My life was changed and marked by meeting Jesus in my guilt and shame and running toward repentance.

Let's begin by refreshing our memory. **Please revisit John 13:1 – 17.**
Verse 1 causes me to stop and ponder about what Jesus must have been thinking and feeling. I don't know about you, but it's difficult for me to peel back my layer of skepticism of Jesus' love toward Judas here. My mind can't comprehend knowing a friend will betray me and still washing his feet, treating him the same as the others even though he wasn't the same; he was the betrayer! What we do know, regardless of how Jesus felt, is the Savior of the World washed his betrayer's feet among men whose hearts were loyal.

Yesterday you recorded verse 2. **Today, I'd like you to write verse 1 below.** You are witnessing how Jesus loved his betrayer.

Let's take this Scripture off the page here by sharing what impacts you about this scene in John 13:1 – 2 between Judas and Jesus.

Let's pick up our luggage and journey over to John 13:18 – 30. **After you've read this passage, write verse 27.**

Earlier, I shared with you a little of my past with Jesus. I'd like to take some time and elaborate. It was during that dark season of life I knew I was not emotionally, physically, or spiritually healthy. I was dying inside, and the glaring giveaway was I stopped experiencing conviction over my sin. In fact, I stopped feeling altogether. Don't get me wrong, feelings don't dictate conviction, but conviction sure does evoke feelings. When I am convicted, I feel something about it, and I make a choice: to continue in the "it" or repent from the "it." At that time, all these feelings had ceased. And, they had been long gone for a while. I had been indulging in sin for so long that I just didn't care anymore. It was in this place that I thought I was fooling everyone and getting away with my sin. The reality was, I was the one being fooled.

I tell you this because I can't help but wonder if this is where Judas' heart was, like mine, long gone before the night of his betrayal. Perhaps he, too, thought he was getting away with sin. Think about it, Jesus said in front of Judas, "One of you will betray me." Doesn't it strike you that Judas didn't feel like he was just caught red handed? How was he not sweating with such nervousness that he didn't blurt out, "Ok, Lord, you caught me! It's me!" Surely Judas wasn't ignorant to Jesus' authority by this point. Unless he was already so deep in his sin that he thought he was fooling everyone — including Jesus. Had Judas stopped feeling conviction over sin, making it impossible for him to understand what Jesus was making so perfectly clear?

This truth can't just sit dead on the page of Scripture. These words have to pierce our heart, so let's enter this scene by recording below a time you stopped experiencing conviction.
*please note: conviction is a result of God's kindness that leads to freedom. Condemnation is the opposite of conviction, which produces shame and, in Christ, there is no condemnation (Romans 2:4; 8:1). Our stories are so interwoven with those in Scripture. **Please summarize John 13:26 – 30 in your own words below.**

Have you ever had sin exposed and chose not to repent? Here we see Judas has been exposed by Jesus, giving him an opportunity to repent but he does not. It is out of great love for us that he leads us to repentance.

Truth for Your Soul: *Or do you show contempt for the riches of his kindness, forbearance and patience, not realizing that God's kindness is intended to lead you to repentance?* (Romans 2:4 ESV)

Read John 13:27, 30 and record Judas' response to his sin being exposed below.

Judas left Jesus that very night. It doesn't seem that Judas had much hesitation about the betrayal of his friend because, once given permission to "go"- through Jesus' complete authority- he went.

From John 13, write down everything about Jesus' response or treatment of Judas that leaves an impact on you.

As help, think back to a time when you felt betrayed by a friend and think about your response to feeling betrayed. Then go back and reread Jesus' interaction and response to Judas. I'll share some responses that left an impact on me to help get you started (see below for my examples):

My Impact:
- Jesus didn't humiliate Judas in front of his friends
- Jesus gave Judas permission to go betray him

Your Impact:

I really wish I could sit down and have coffee with Jesus and talk to him about this because it is so unlike culture. We can miss so much if we read John 13 without utilizing how we are created by our Creator: to feel, express, engage, and interact with this grand narrative.

Let's set up our tents here for the night and end today by revisiting
1 Corinthians 13:4 – 7 and record below how Jesus showed love for Judas (as seen in John 13).
Keep that spark of creativity lit until our next lesson because tomorrow's journey takes endurance!

Journal Space

Day 3

Jesus Loves the Betrayer & Denier

*

Today's Focus: *Search me, God, and know my heart; test me and know my anxious thoughts. See if there is any offensive way in me, and lead me in the way everlasting.* (Psalm 139:23 – 24 NIV)

Judas took control of his life rather than trusting his Lord. He walked with Jesus through his entire ministry, being a first-hand witness to the numerous miracles Jesus performed. In other words, Judas knew better than to do anything but trust Jesus with his desires and his life. Oh, how history seems to repeat itself. We aren't all that different than Bible times as we'd like to think. Sure, our wardrobe has changed, but our hearts are prone to wander all the same.

There was a time in life I had been trying to play tug-o-war with God over control of my life. Here's the real deal with that though, God is in control regardless of how I felt, so he was no active participant in this game. I was deep in this game all on my own, but I didn't see that clearly. Sin does that, blinds us from seeing what Jesus makes so perfectly clear. I could have just dropped the rope and ran to him, but I didn't because that tight grip and the blisters starting to form made me feel tough. What I didn't know was those blisters that made me feel tough were infected with pride and oozing with arrogance, that I was nearly dying and had no idea. You see, the Enemy thought it had me for good and was laughing at me all along. The reality is, Jesus was about to perform one of the grandest miracles my eyes have ever seen—the saving of my soul.

What about you? On the last page for today, is a diagram for you to complete. The purpose of this is to spend time with the Lord, asking him to reveal areas of your life you've been unwilling, like I once was, to surrender to him. You may have a few that come to mind right away but don't just stop there. We tend to be fickle creatures and not hang on for the full healing as if to trade in our five-course meal for the "fast food" version of healing. Full healing is what we are after in this exercise, and it may take some searching, prodding, and probing (ouch) to reveal our hearts in the most true form, vulnerable. Judas missed this type of healing, but you don't have to.

Truth for Your Soul: *Truly I tell you, if you have faith as small as a mustard seed, you can say to this mountain, 'Move from here to there,' and it will move. Nothing will be impossible for you.* (Matthew 17:20 NIV)

Directions for Tug-o-War Diagram (see next page):

- **On the far-left side** above the line, draw a stick figure. This stick figure will represent you.

- **On the far-right side** above the line, draw a cross to represent God. The line represents the rope.

- **Below the cross**, I want you to jot down all the ways God's been faithful to you in the past. This is your history with him, your personal proof of his faithfulness. If there is any Scripture that comes to mind, record it here.

- **Below the stick figure**, jot down when God began to draw you into a relationship with him. Add any details surrounding life events that might be valuable.

- **Above the rope**, I want you to list all the areas of your life you've been fighting for control (family, comfort, fear, success, job, school, etc.). Please do not shy away from being specific here.

- Finally, **below the rope**, confess and repent of each area of life that makes you crave control rather than trusting Jesus as if you are playing tug-o-war. Like David, in the book of Psalm, call and cry out to God as you pour out your heart's desires, confessing your hurts, and trusting he will bring full healing. Pouring out your hurts and pain for the sake of soul healing will never be a wasted effort.

Truth for Your Soul: *"In repentance and rest is your salvation…"* (Isaiah 30:15 NIV)

This is a necessary stop on our journey. Rest up through repentance with your Savior. Tomorrow we embark a little lighter as we leave some baggage at this stop.

Day 4

Jesus Loves the Betrayer & Denier

*

Today's Focus: *Bear fruit in keeping with repentance.* (Matthew 3:8 ESV)

You made it through day three of this study, and I think it's safe to say you are officially immersed in the Scripture. If you are feeling a little tired of all the reading, writing, and reflecting being required of you, good! You are on the right track because what is going on is you are engaging with Scripture and that takes a careful, slower process than most things we do in our day-to-day living.

We have invested our first week of study to around the time of Jesus' betrayal and crucifixion. These last few days we have focused much of our attention on Jesus and Judas. At this point, you may be seeing some similarities between you and Judas, which is why it's important to say if you have the Holy Spirit living inside of you, Satan cannot enter you like he did Judas. Please be sure to implant this truth in your mind so it can start to sprout more truth without getting entangled in the weeds of lies from the Enemy.

Read John 13:1 – 30 allowing your mind to reflect back on Judas and your ears to perk up as you go meet Peter.

Judas and Peter were both Jesus' disciples and friends. They shared something else in common too: betrayal of Jesus. However, the two men do not share the same response to their betrayal. In fact, their responses were drastically different from each other. One led to life and the other to death. Today and tomorrow you will witness the striking difference of repentance and remorse through the lives of Judas and Peter.

Let's do some preparation before we enter this scene in John 13:31 – 38, ok? To properly prepare, think of someone who is dear to you, someone the Lord has used as a compass pointing to the Truth for you. In fact, for the sake of clarity during this activity, let's just refer to this individual as "your compass." These types of people come in different forms by way of a mentor or friend, spiritual mother or teacher. For me, it was my mom before she died. Today, it's a conglomeration of women, but for the sake of this activity, I'll narrow it down to one, Lori. Now it's your turn. Do you have your compass in mind? Once you do, find a place to get comfortable, quiet the noise, and prepare your mind for some reflection as you think about the following questions:

*please note: If you do not have a compass in your life, consider someone you dearly love whose absence would change the trajectory of your life.

What makes them so special to you (they can't be replaced because their touch on your life has been a personal gift from God)?

Think back on your history together, what are some of your most memorable moments?

Continuing to think back on your history together, think of a time(s) you laughed together and remember why you laughed. Retell the story in your mind. If you find yourself smiling at the memory, good! What do you love about this person? What does she love about you?

What makes her different than all the rest of the people in your life?

*What would her absence mean to you? How would
you be affected by her absence in your life? What
would be lost for you if her presence was no more?*

As you hold these reflections in your mind, **open
your Bible to John 13 and read verses 31 – 38** and
do your best to picture this scene.

Pulling from your reflections with your personal
compass, how do you think Peter felt toward Jesus?
Share your thoughts below.

I can't help but wonder what Peter must have felt
after hearing from Jesus he would deny him just as

Jesus was facing his death. Can you imagine how you may feel if your personal compass told you that you would do the same? Scripture doesn't tell us what Peter or Jesus was thinking or feeling here, so we are left to wonder. However, what we do know is they were both real human beings, flesh and bone, and Peter's feelings were vocal as if to say, "No! I would die with you before I ever had to say goodbye to you."

Share your thoughts on Peter's response to Jesus, in verse 37, below.

As your conclusion for today, record the scene between Peter and Jesus in your own words (John 13:36 – 38).

Truth for Your Soul: *Having loved his own who were in the world, he loved them to the end.* (John 13:1b ESV)

Jesus loved Peter until the very end. He is doing the same for you on this very journey and until you make it safely home to spend eternity with him.

Day 5

Jesus Loves the Betrayer & Denier

*

Today's Focus: *Godly sorrow brings repentance that leads to salvation and leaves no regret, but worldly sorrow brings death.* (2 Corinthians 7:10 NIV)

I'm going to bring it back to high school days and whip out the good ol' Venn Diagram to compare and contrast Judas' and Peter's responses to their own betrayal—after all, this is the one comparison we don't want to misunderstand.

We have spent the last week getting to know these men and their relationships with Jesus. Now, it is time to bring it all together and produce our take-away from the week: Jesus loved both these men and yet only one experienced repentance, leading to the saving of his soul.

Today, my hope is you see the blatant difference be-tween repentance and remorse through the lives of Judas and Peter and then choose to walk as Peter did because this is your salvation. Below, I have listed the directions for the diagram you will complete.

Directions for the Venn Diagram:
- Locate the diagram on the last page of today's study.
- **You will label the left circle "Judas."** This will be where you record everything you witness in Scripture of his betrayal of Jesus.
- Next, you will **label the right circle "Peter."** This is where you record everything you witness in Scripture related to his denial of Jesus.
- Finally, **the middle will be where you record similarities between the two men** revealed in Scripture.

Scripture passages to reference for this exercise: John 13, John 18 (Peter's denial), and Luke 22 (Judas agrees to betray Jesus).

Truth for Your Soul: *O Lord, all my longing is before you; my sighing is not hidden from you.* (Psalm 38:9 NIV)

After you complete this exercise, you will be staring in the face of true repentance. The beauty about your Savior is he isn't going to force you to repent but give you a choice. The choice you make will either bring life or it will bring death; there is no in-between when it comes to salvation.

As today comes to a close, it is my deepest desire that the truths we talked about today—and the entire week—collide with your heart and produce a desire for true repentance. The choice is yours, but the depth this study will take you depends on it! We continue to embark in week two by focusing in on the life of Peter.

Truth for Your Soul: *"In returning and rest is you shall be saved..."* (Isaiah 30:15 ESV). I love how the NIV translates this verse as well, *"In repentance and rest is your salvation..."*

Journey on, fellow sojourner!

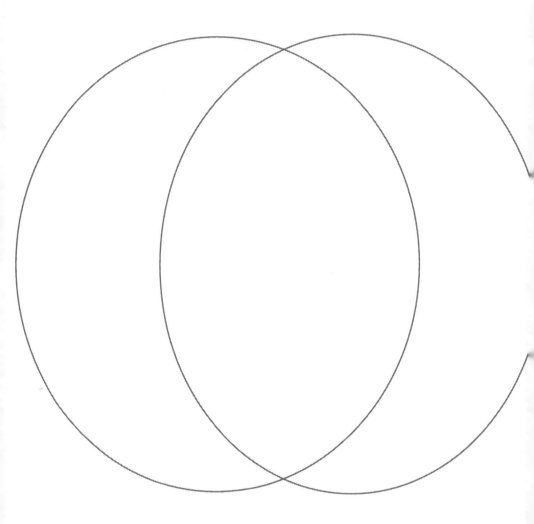

Oh, Goodness the Bible Study

Week Two

Reflecting on God's Goodness

Day 1

Result of Repentance

*

Today's Focus: *"My grace is sufficient for you, for my power is made perfect in weakness." Therefore I will boast all the more gladly about my weaknesses, so that Christ's power may rest on me. That is why, for Christ's sake, I delight in weaknesses, in insults, in hardships, in persecutions, in difficulties. For when I am weak, then I am strong.* (2 Corinthians 12:9 – 10 NIV)

The cornerstone of last week was repentance versus remorse and Jesus' unmoved love through it all. This week, we are going to journey out of life with Judas and completely focus on doing life like Peter: choosing repentance. Oh, Peter. I sure have a soft spot in my heart for him because I can relate with him in many ways. As we embark on this journey with Peter, I hope you get lost in the story as if this were you and Jesus.

Please read John 13:31 – 38 and summarize the scene between Peter and Jesus in your own words.

I know what it's like to lose someone you love and have lived life with. I know the pain of their physical absence, so when I read this narrative between Peter and Jesus, my heart can't help but go there to that place of pain, knowing the one you love is no longer going to walk this life with you. Can you ponder upon what Peter may have been thinking and feeling at this time? **Share your thoughts below.**

Luke 22:31 – 38 also records this same scene, so take some time to read this passage. **What strikes you about how John's focus differs from Luke's?**

From Luke, we know that Satan asked to sift Peter like wheat, but what does this mean? We can read this until we are blue in the face, but it doesn't mean anything until it penetrates our soul, so let's layer in some more details to try and connect with Peter. A basic Google search gives the definition of "sift":

> To Sift: examine thoroughly so as to isolate that which is most important or useful, separate something, especially something to be discarded, from something else, put through a sieve so as to remove lumps or large particles.
> *Synonyms: look through, inspect, examine, scrutinize, dissect, get rid of (Oxford Dictionary 2019)*

Satan asked to sift Peter, scrutinize and get rid of his faith. Jesus allowed it because he would come back and strengthen his brother's faith through it. **Write Luke 22:32 below.**

Let's kick up some creativity here and use those beautiful minds God created us with by thinking about what Peter might have been thinking and feeling after he was told he would be sifted by Satan? **Share your thoughts below.**

In our weakness, He is strong. However, Peter had yet to know how weak he truly was. This is a place I have to remember Scripture as a whole and not in part. It would be easy to feel connected to Peter as you think about ways you've been sifted and felt abandoned by God. I spent nearly five years of my life in that place, so I am familiar with it down to the wallpaper of lies that plaster my mind. For that sake alone, let's draw on Romans 8:28 to help in understanding God's goodness in the sifting (we will talk in greater detail about this in the weeks to come).

Truth for Your Soul: *And we know that in all things God works for the good of those who love him, who have been called according to his purpose.* (Romans 8:28 NIV)

Dear one, "God knows your faith, your weakness, your love and -- if you are a believer -- how He will transform you to make you like His Son. Your life is 'hidden with Christ in God.' He loves you now as though you have already reached the perfection He has promised" (Bible Study Fellowship, Lesson 18). Satan can sift you only if it will be worked for your good. Peter could trust Jesus with that and so can you.

Here is where the denials come in and the rooster crows; and we remember what Satan meant for harm, the Lord meant for good. **Fill in the diagram below by summarizing, in your own words, each of the four scenes from the Gospels of Peter's three denials**.

Peter's Denial

Matthew 26:69 – 75

Mark 14:66 – 71

Luke 22:54 – 71

John 18:15 – 26

When we merge all these Scriptures together, it is then we receive a complete picture of what God wanted us to know about this scene. I hope you exercise your right to soak in all the Lord has for you here in these passages.

We are going to settle down for the day by looking at the effect all these denials had on Peter. Let's bear up under some Scripture one last time. Don't tire out on me now!

Read Matthew 26:75 below.

> *Suddenly, Jesus' words flashed through Peter's mind: 'Before the rooster crows, you will deny three times that you even know me.' And he went away, weeping bitterly.* (ESV)

Next, please **record Luke 22:61 – 62 below.**

Peter was so broken over his sin that he left, weeping bitterly. He was on the road to repentance. God was going to work his bitter weeping for Peter's good even if it didn't feel good to Peter at the time. Peter's life was forever marked that day, and it would be a marking that would strengthen others. Please don't confuse markings of God as scars of neglect. Peter wasn't scarred by Satan from his sifting but instead healed and marked by God. You carry the markings of your Savior as well, dear one. These are markings that will carry you through the rest of this journey. We continue to embark tomorrow.

Day 2

Result of Repentance

*

Today's Focus: *Instead of your shame you will receive a double portion, and instead of disgrace you
will rejoice in your inheritance. And so you will inherit a double portion in your land, and everlasting
joy will be yours.* (Isaiah 61:7 NIV)

In the end, Peter lived up to the meaning of his name
well. In fact, let's look for ourselves at what John
wants us to know about Peter's response to his own
denial of Jesus. Before we do this, let's refresh our
memory on how Jesus predicted Peter would live up
to his name. **Please read and record Luke 22:32
below.**

Jesus had faith that Peter would turn back. After all, Peter means a "rock or stone" (Hitchcock 1871), but there wasn't just a singular purpose to his sifting. In fact, this sifting would multiply and impact his brothers by strengthening them. Instead of shame, Peter received a double portion; instead of disgrace, he would rejoice in his inheritance. Everlasting joy was his because he chose a repentance story.

Let's meet over at John 20 today and see what John wanted us to know about Peter's reaction to going to Jesus after his denial of him. **Read John 20:1 – 10 and record anything that strikes you regarding Peter's response to Mary Magdalene.**

Before we leave this scene, **read Luke 24:11 – 12** below and witness something remarkable from Peter. This is the same scene we find in John 20 but with some added detail.

> *But they ("the disciples and others") did not believe the women, because their words*

seemed to them like nonsense. Peter, however, got up and ran to the tomb.

While everyone else doubted, Peter ran straight to find Jesus. This is the part of the story that gets me every time… though he denied Jesus, he couldn't hold himself back from running to him—to see him with his own eyes.

Guilt makes us want to hide, repentance makes us want to run to our Savior. Peter didn't care what grown men did or didn't do, he just cared about getting to his Savior and seeing him with his own eyes, as fast as possible. **Repentance has a focus: Jesus. Guilt has a focus: self.**

What about you? Are you living in guilt, hiding from your Savior, or in repentance, running to him? As you think on Peter, **ponder these questions for yourself and start recording some thoughts below**.

continue pondering:

Jesus is your Savior and if you have chosen to follow him, you have been given a name—His Beloved—and it means dearly loved. Your inheritance is rich, and you can have a glimpse of what it looks like in Isaiah 61. **Read this passage below and circle any part of your inheritance that has an impact on you.**

The Year of the Lord's Favor
The Spirit of the Sovereign Lord is on me,
because the Lord has anointed me
to proclaim good news to the poor.
He has sent me to bind up the brokenhearted,
to proclaim freedom for the captives
and release from darkness for the prisoners,[a]
to proclaim the year of the Lord's favor
and the day of vengeance of our God,
to comfort all who mourn,

and provide for those who grieve in Zion—
to bestow on them a crown of beauty
instead of ashes,
the oil of joy
instead of mourning,

and a garment of praise
instead of a spirit of despair.
They will be called oaks of righteousness,
a planting of the Lord
for the display of his splendor.
They will rebuild the ancient ruins
and restore the places long devastated;
they will renew the ruined cities
that have been devastated for generations.

Strangers will shepherd your flocks;
foreigners will work your fields and vineyards.

And you will be called priests of the Lord,
you will be named ministers of our God.
You will feed on the wealth of nations,
and in their riches you will boast.

Instead of your shame
you will receive a double portion,
and instead of disgrace
you will rejoice in your inheritance.
And so you will inherit a double portion in your
land,
and everlasting joy will be yours.

"For I, the Lord, love justice;
I hate robbery and wrongdoing.
In my faithfulness I will reward my people
and make an everlasting covenant with them.

Their descendants will be known among the nations

and their offspring among the peoples.
All who see them will acknowledge
that they are a people the Lord has blessed. "

I delight greatly in the Lord;
my soul rejoices in my God.
For he has clothed me with garments of salvation
and arrayed me in a robe of his righteousness,
as a bridegroom adorns his head like a priest,
and as a bride adorns herself with her jewels.

For as the soil makes the sprout come up
and a garden causes seeds to grow,
so the Sovereign Lord will make righteousness
and praise spring up before all nations.

Before we end today, I'd like you to bring along what we witnessed today, from Peter, as you continue to ponder your repentance story. Below are some questions to help get you started, but don't feel like you have to stop there. The aim today would be that you jot down anything that gives life to your repentance story, which we will start writing tomorrow. Write away!

> *Please note: If you do not feel like you have a repentance story, do not feel discouraged or abandoned during this portion of the study. First, our repentance isn't based on our feelings, so keep that in mind. Second, a heart of repentance can start today. There is a no one-size-fits-all story here and that's the beauty of

it! It's when we collide all our stories that we get a glimpse of the fullness of our God.

Truth for Your Soul: *Search me, God, and know my heart; test me and know my anxious thoughts. See if there is any offensive way in me, and lead me in the way everlasting.* (Psalm 139:23 – 24 NIV)

Pondering Your Repentance Story

• Are there areas of your life you know you're living in that are wrong, but you are unwilling to do anything different about? What are those areas? What impact have they made on your life?

• Are there areas of your life you want to break free from the bondage of sin but you don't know how?

- Will you ask the Lord to change your heart to desire what pleases him? AND do you trust he is able and will see this through in your life? How do you know you trust him?

- How have you seen remorse without conviction take a toll on your life?

- In what ways have you experienced conviction, and how has it changed your life?

Store up these treasures from heaven where moth and rust cannot destroy and Satan cannot take away (Matthew 6:20 NIV). If You are tiring out here, ask God for help to "stand firm" (Ephesians 6 NIV). I'll meet you tomorrow at the point of Peter's weakness. Until then, dear one...

Day 3

Result of Repentance

*

If I was told when I was eighteen that my life would soon mirror those I once harshly judged, I would have denied it quicker than prey running from its predator. I truly thought I was a good girl and a good Christian, solid as a rock, who would not budge even in the face of temptation. Now, don't get me wrong here, I knew I was a sinning-machine that made all sorts of wrong choices, but I never made "those" choices. You know, the really bad ones that really bad people make (or so my old way of thinking went). It's like that one sin we hold over others' heads as if it's the worst one in the world, and if ever committed, you are done for. I took pride in being the good girl and not making mistakes, at least not ones that would publicly denounce me of my throne of pride. I held so much stock in being viewed as a "good girl" who made good choices that people could look up to. It wasn't just that I took pride in it, but that it became something that defined me, so when that came into question because of terrible choices I made, I fell apart. This was my identity, so I never would have believed who I would become even if I had been told, much like Peter was when Jesus told him of his impending denial.

I can't help but wonder if that is how Peter felt after Jesus said to him that he would deny knowing Jesus. Here is a man who has walked with Jesus during his ministry, he loved him and was loved by him. He was a friend to him, he was a follower. Jesus was his teacher, he went with him everywhere, even to the cross! I can't help but think he had to have looked at Jesus as if to say, "You've got to be kidding me? I've walked with you for this long, what on earth makes you think I'd deny you now of all times?!" Peter had yet to know just how weak he was, even so, Jesus loved Peter in his weakness and imperfection just as he loves you.

Today's Focus: *That is why, for Christ's sake, I delight in weaknesses, in insults, in hardships, in persecutions, in difficulties. For when I am weak, then I am strong.* (2 Corinthians 12:10 NIV)

After getting to know Peter, this verse has some feeling behind it, some meaning making it more than inspiration but a reality for my life (and yours too). Peter was weak, he just didn't know it yet, but soon he would delight in it because it was in that weakness his faith would be made strong and he would come back to truth. In doing so, he would strengthen his brothers, and his coming back continues to strengthen others, it's strengthening you today.

Write Luke 22:31 – 32 below.

Hold on to these words for a second while we head over to Romans 8. **Please write Romans 8:28 below.**

What if your pain in the sifting had purpose? What if the sin you committed was the very thing that led to your repentance? If you truly believed God works everything out for the good of those

"who have been called according to his purpose,"
how would the way you lived life be different?
Share your thoughts below.

There seems to be this question that always surfaces
in times of sifting and that is, "Is God really good?"
As we begin to unfold God's goodness, we uncover
his unmoved love for us. We saw that with Judas and
now we see that with Peter.

We are just about to round the corner to our final
destination for today, but before we arrive, let's
make two final stops at John 13 and Luke 22:31 -
32. Once you arrive to each destination, take your
time and look around, getting familiar with the scene
in each passage. **When you are ready, record all
the ways Jesus showed love to Peter even though
Jesus knew Peter would soon deny him. Does
anything strike you or grab your attention?
Write it out.** Enjoy your time at each place, and I'll

meet you at your final destination: My Journey to Repentance, journal entry from April 24, 2010.

Journal Entry from 4.24.2010
a piece of my repentance story
First Stop: the unpaved, rocky road of bitterness

God,
Just send me to hell already. I am filled up with so much hate and bitterness and I don't see any way of healing from this agony. I'm going to drown in this place, aren't I? I'm done for, too tired to tread this water any more. Let me just die here. I hate myself, who I've become.

All I want to know from you is, why? Why on earth did you let me get this far into this sin. I know I wanted you to leave me alone, but Lord, you knew better than me and now look... how is anything good going to come from this, from me? All this time, all these years, and it's turned to this ... I've traded you in for what feels like a one-night stand, and now I can't seem to forgive myself, believe in your forgiveness. Your word says you forgive, renew, and restore, but can you really do that with this, through me? Oh Lord, I hate myself, who I've become.

I am so done with the judgement sounds of religion. Is this really what Christianity is made of? I feel like a spectacle. Almost like they are just watching me drown and throwing a Bible verse at me as if to provide a floatation device—when really I need some-

one willing to dive in and tread these dangerous waters with me. But they don't and they won't because this time, even they know, I'm in too deep. See, I'm a mess, and I don't need to know what I'm doing is wrong, but how to survive in this place of knowing but not believing. Oh Lord, how do I believe when I feel like I'm drowning in all this sin?

Why can't I just feel loved by you again? Why can't I desire you again? Why can't I feel you near? Oh Lord, what has become of me?

Maria

What looked like a hopeless situation was the beginning of my undoing my skewed theology and regluing of a clear understanding of his goodness. Here comes the healing.

Day 4

Result of Repentance

*

Yesterday I shared with you an unrestrained piece of my repentance story from 2010. It was an intensely frightening season, to be frank. I had come face to face with my own weakness coming off the heels of thinking I was strong. That created all sorts of identity crises for me. Like Peter, I had no idea just how weak I was. In fact, I'd go as far to say I really thought I was rock solid on the faith front.

Pride, dear one, is the ultimate creeper and it is sneaky. It likes to creep up and disguise itself as humility, and if we aren't careful, we fall victim and the fall is hard and deep. This was once my life, so I know it to be true.

Here's the freedom sound of all of this though: God completes the good work he starts in you and me as we continue to abide and follow him. There was a good work started in you as a Christ follower, so he will bring it to completion just as he did for Peter. Jesus loved Peter deeply, even though he knew Peter would deny him, quite frankly a betrayal in my book. Yet, Jesus doesn't think like us, does he? He sees us for who we are, incomplete until he makes us complete, and there is no perfection until we reach Heaven. Jesus loved Peter in his weakness and imperfection.

Yesterday you recorded ways Jesus loved Peter as seen in John 13 and Luke 22. I hope you took time to really sit and soak in those passages. If you haven't yet completed it, please do before moving any further on today's study because it is a necessary preparation for today.

Like we did with Peter, we are now going to record how Jesus has shown love to you over the course of your life. To do this, I created a simple diagram with a checklist that sections off your life. **By going in chronological order, you will fill in the diagram below by recording ways you can remember experiencing God's faithfulness in your life.**

I reserved this exercise for week two because we needed time to meet our Savior and witness his unmoved love first. If your heart is still unsettled about God's love for you, you may find this exercise challenging. In that case, pray and give this activity some time. I want you to still complete this activity, but with prayer and patience and pondering. You may not be able to finish it in one sitting but throughout the week. Challenge yourself to come back to this activity because remembering his goodness personally builds faith.

Before you begin, it would be wise to remind your-self of the definition of "love" that we are working with. **Read 1 Corinthians 13 and revisit week one and two for additional refreshers.** During this ex-ercise, ask your Heavenly Father to help you learn and see ways he has been faithful to you that you may not be seeing. Once you finish here, meet me over at our final destination for the day, the second stop of my repentance story.

Check off once you have completed each section on the diagram:

•Childhood (the age you first remember until about
  10)   _____

•Adolescence (about 11 – 19)   _____

•Young adult (about 20 – 25)   _____

*use the line on the next page to begin recording from each section of our life.

Diagram:

Journal Entry from 6.12.2010
a piece of my repentance journey
Second Stop: recalling God's faithfulness

Heavenly Father,
Today you have given me a peace and I truly have
no idea where it is coming from. Every part of my
life is suffocating me with shame and guilt but not
today…today you've allowed my soul to rest from
this haunting.

Today I've been able to eat and enjoy the taste of
food, get dressed and ready, get out of the house,
worked out and showered, and smiled. Today I expe-
rienced joy and my face showed it for the first time
in a long time.

Today I am soaking in Psalm 145:5 – 7,

> *They speak of the glorious splendor of your*
> *majesty—and I will meditate on your won-*
> *derful works. They tell of the power of your*
> *awesome works—and I will proclaim your*
> *great deeds. They celebrate your abundant*
> *goodness and joyfully sing of your right-*
> *eousness.* (NIV)

But my question to You is how am I supposed to
"celebrate your abundant goodness" and "joyfully
sing of your righteousness" when I feel so very un-

worthy? Lord, people who know my sin by name judge me harshly, so how can I feel I can worship you without judgment (from you and others)? I have tried to shut the mouth of my enemies by not taking to heart what they say, but I failed.

I didn't know life would turn out like this, that I would turn out like this. I've completely blown it! You are calling me to rise up, but, Lord, I can barely look up. "You have overcome the world" so please overcome this bondage to my sin. My mind now recalls your past faithfulness as if my momentary amnesia has been healed.

Thank you Father,
Maria

Day 5

Result of Repentance

*

It's a new and beautiful day to embark! Yesterday may have felt heavy and that's ok because it was meant to be. In fact, if you didn't feel anything as you recorded God's faithfulness, just did the work to check it off, I'm going to ask you to consider pushing pause here and going back and taking some time to feel something about this…joy, frustration, doubt, assurance, confusion, longing. Find the feeling and then tell him, asking him to help you know how to trust that he is going to finish the good work in you (Philippians 1:6). If you experienced nothing but complete assurance and joy, thank him.

Feelings should not dictate our truth but Truth, most definitely, evokes feelings and trying to stifle those feelings is like trying to tell the sun not to shine. This is who you were created to be: a being with feelings! If we are uneasy about the fact that God created us this way, how on earth can we digest his truth for us personally? I hope you journey back to yesterday and feel something, anything, about God's faithfulness, telling him those feelings and asking him to help you submit those feelings to Christ.

Truth for Your Soul: *We demolish arguments and every pretension that sets itself up against the knowledge of God, and we take captive every thought to make it obedient to Christ.* (2 Corinthians 10:5 NIV)

Yesterday, I left you with some writing prompts to begin reflecting on your story, and you can always go back and add to those. If you haven't completed yesterday's activity, you might consider completing it before you start writing your story today.

The past two days you got to be an eye-witness to my repentance story, and today you will record your own. Whether writing is your "thing" or not, it is always good to record the Lord's faithfulness in our lives through our testimony. So, consider this your training ground for when you go and share your story with someone else. But before you begin writing, I want to be sure you have "done all your research" and really asked God if there is more to your story you have yet to write down, parts you aren't seeing, or pieces you are missing. With that, I decided to share my recordings to yesterday's questions with you as if I was back in the year 2010. Feel free to read and maybe this will trigger some reminders of missing pieces to your story. Enjoy this part of the journey! He sure is enjoying you at this very moment.

Truth for Your Soul: *Therefore, if anyone is in Christ, the new creation has come: The old has gone, the new is here!* (2 Corinthians 5:17 NIV)

- Are there areas of my life I know I'm living in that are wrong but I'm unwilling to do anything different about? What are those areas? What impact have they made on your life?

> *Yes.*

> *I need to be liked, be loved, be seen, be valued. I thrive here, I crave this feeling, so I chase it hard like a drug. Once I used to want and desire these things, but now I've tasted it and have become addicted to it. These things I do, these things I think, these things I cling to help my addiction stay alive. I do not want to let go of these because they are mine, they make me feel seen and valued. I live in the tension of knowing I am not honoring or obeying God and yet not wanting to let go and surrender.*

> *The impact this has made on my life has left me confused. I chase after this way of life because it once satisfied, but I'm getting bored with it, so I continue to have to feed on more, which poses a threat. At some point, I can only feed this addiction for so long before it becomes deadly, be-*

fore others find out, before I become the addiction. I know this and yet I still choose to stay.

- Are there areas of my life I want to break free from the bondage of sin, but I don't know how?

  I cannot imagine desiring anything different to this thing I crave that so opposes living for God, so yes. If it's possible that I could stop craving these things and truly crave God, I'd like to know about it, but as of now, I'm having a hard time believing that is possible.

- Will I ask the Lord to change my heart to desire what pleases him? AND do I trust he is able and will see this through in my life?

  I am willing, but no I do not trust or believe that this can be seen through to completion in my life. Honestly, it has less to do about what God can do and more that I know myself... I'm too prone to wonder, I'm too addicted to this way of living, I crave it all too much.

- How have I demonstrated remorse without conviction in my life?

  I suppose right now. I don't like where I am in my life. I'm not happy or fulfilled here, not really. There are times I feel happy and times I feel fulfilled, but that always seems to be mixed with feeling dirty and worthless. I hate what I'm doing, and I don't want to be in this addiction, but I stay because, well, because I'm addicted.

• In what ways have I experienced conviction, and how has it changed my life?

I don't know...

I am aware that with conviction comes repentance comes change.

The idea of changing this way of living that I've come so accustom to seems impossible. I don't know how to change or turn from this way of living when I am this addicted to it.

I suppose I'm feeling the conviction about my lack of conviction.

Whew. Praise the Lord he makes us new creations because I can't imagine living that life of loneliness, emptiness, shame, and guilt (to that degree) ever again! I know this type of pondering and reflecting can feel weary and hard and repetitive, but we are aiming for heart change, not a completed study, right? It's ok that things are hard to complete as long as we hang on for the full healing. Will you keep going in this study with me? Will you commit to finishing this thing strong? If so, let's keep moving forward, on to some healing!

Is there a time in your life you stopped experiencing conviction? Maybe you are a new believer, so you spent many years like this, and conviction is a new concept to you. If you feel unclear on what "conviction" means, consider thinking back to the comparison we did of Peter and Judas. Both men had a reason for regret but only one experienced godly conviction. It's God's kindness that leads to conviction, and we saw that with Peter.

Now, you write! As you put your story to pen and paper and give it life and meaning, please remember one key concept: repentance is more than simply feeling bad or experiencing remorse about a behavior, but a deliberate choice to turn from regret. In fact, as you write, it might benefit you to go back to our Venn Diagram we completed in week one and note the differences between remorse and repentance.

Enough from me, now it's your turn to take the initiative from here. The depth of this exercise is solely your choice.

> *Maybe you don't have a repentance story yet because you haven't repented. Been there, lived that. For you, I'd like to encourage you to write what your repentance story would look like by creating a character and writing her repentance story. She will have your story, maybe additional details (get creative) and*

write her journey to repentance by relying on what we've discussed about God's love and goodness. After you've finished, go back and read your story as if this character were you because it can be, and I believe it will be.

I've already titled it for you, all you need is to fill in your name. Today I cover you in prayer as I leave you to be alone with your Savior here. I will join you again tomorrow.

_____ Journey to Repentance

Oh, Goodness the Bible Study

Week Three

Reflecting on God's to You

Day 1

Is God Really Good

*

Today's Focus: *I am the true vine, and my Father is the gardener. He cuts off every branch in me that bears no fruit, while every branch that does bear fruit he prunes so that it will be even more fruitful.* (John 15:1 – 2 NIV)

After my parents died, I spent five years haunted by this question, "Is God good?" I knew the Bible said he was, so it had to be true, but I felt that there was too much evidence against his goodness to really believe it to be true for my life.

I wasn't content living with this lingering question. I had to understand and see his goodness in my life, not just know it was true. So, in an effort to do different than I once would have, I stayed and pressed in a little more to him. I asked the questions, felt the feelings brought on by those questions, and asked him to show me his goodness in my life—with an expectation that he would answer. Whether the answer satisfied my longing or not, I just had to know if it was true.

As we navigate through this next portion of our journey, I will share more of this with you. Here's the deal, we can learn how to talk the Christian talk saying things like "God is good," we may even believe that we believe it but then "that" thing happens. You know, that one untouchable, the one thing that, if taken away, shakes the very core of who you are, bringing everything you thought you knew about God into question.

We can do surface in our relationship with God. Surface is easy because it feels good for a time, it's enjoyable because there's no challenges to work through, because it's all surface. Often, it's people with a more surface relationship that say things like "God is good" when what they really mean is, "God is good because my life feels good, looks good, and is enjoyable." I have come to find it's people with some depth about them that say "God is good" from their gut, their core, sometimes through tears, because they know…"this might possibly be the worst thing I've ever felt, nearly taking me out, and it could all happen again but even still… God is good." I've been both these people.

After the plane crash that took my parents' lives, I had the opportunity to stay surface in my relationship with Christ. After all, it is my choice, yet the plane crash was this boulder right in front of me as to remind me, "Girlfriend, you are going to have to get down and dirty if you are going to move passed this one — there is nothing surface that can happen here," so I chose depth.

Week three focuses on having a relationship with Christ that has some depth, some guts and wits about it. Before we go seeking depth, there has to be exposure and examination of the true condition of our heart in its most natural state, vulnerable. A doctor wouldn't go into a surgery without knowledge of the problem, just taking a "stab at it" in hopes of making the correct first incision. Instead, it takes consultations to understand concerns and symptoms, imaging, and in some cases more testing. It is no different here. Your "doctor" is your Heavenly Father, and it would do you well to allow him to examine your heart before we dive into John 15.

Write Psalm 139:23 – 24 below and ask the Lord to expose your true belief to the question, *"Do you, (insert your name), believe God is good?"*

After you've considered the above, read John 15:1 – 18.

Next, follow the directions listed on the next few pages to fill in the diagram below.

Vine & Branches Diagram:

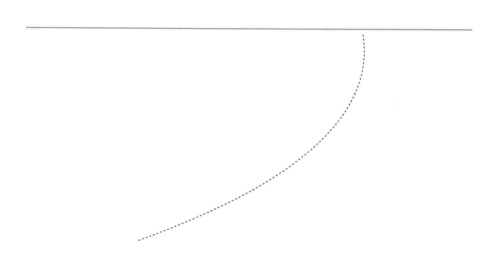

Directions for the Diagram:

In small print, write the names of our main characters for this study in the appropriate places on the diagram. We will be filling in some more detail so be sure to write small. Please check each piece of detail you filled out as you go:

Main Characters:

_____   God, the Gardener: The cross

_____   Jesus, the True Vine: The green line

_____   Christians, the Branches: The green curve coming off the vine

Next, finish up the diagram by writing out the purpose of each (the Gardner, True Vine, branch) near each image. Yours may read something like:

- The Gardner: keep the True Vine healthy by pruning and cutting off the dead branches so the True Vine is producing much fruit
- True Vine: to produce much fruit from the branches
- Branches: to bear lasting fruit

This is the foundation for the rest of the study. Today, we are taking Scripture off the pages, laying out the foundation with the purpose to fully enter into this grand narrative tomorrow. With that said, let's continue building on our foundation.

Now we build on the foundation of the branches. Things can get really wonky here if we abandon Scripture and start telling our own story. For instance, we know that Scripture says the branches' job is to bear lasting fruit. As pride-bearing humans, we can really muck up the definition of "lasting fruit." We tend to think that our good works, success, level of tolerance of mean people, etc., are lasting fruit, and while those things are good, I'd like to suggest that is not all Scripture is referring to when talking about "lasting fruit."

Let's see what Scripture has to say about this type of fruit by visiting "The Fruit of the Spirit." **Read Galatians 5:22 – 23 and list out each fruit of the Spirit below**:

- L

- J

- P

- P

- K

- G

- F

- G

- S

Once you are done listing the fruit of the Spirit here, go back to our diagram of the Vine and Branches, on page 56, and draw some fruit off the vine—get creative! Then, inside the fruit drawn, label each one by listing the Fruit of the Spirit. In total, you will have nine pieces of fruit drawn off your branch.

Our foundation laying is coming to completion! Let's finish up by looking over our nicely laid foundation by answering the following questions. Please answer in the space provided after each question.

- Who is the True Vine?

• Who is the Gardener?

• Who are the branches?

• What is the role of the Gardener?

• What is the role of the True Vine?

• What is the role of the branches?

In preparation for tomorrow, read John 15 and Romans 8:28 one last time. As you do, consider pondering what beliefs (wrong or right) you have

about God's goodness. This is the place true soul healing can happen—the exposing of our true heart condition.

Day 2

Is God Really Good

*

Today's Focus: *I am the true vine, and my Father is the gardener. He cuts off every branch in me that bears no fruit, while every branch that does bear fruit he prunes so that it will be even more fruitful… This is to my Father's glory, that you bear much fruit, showing yourselves to be my disciples.* (John 15:1 – 2, 8 NIV)

Heavenly Father, today marks the day _____ begins to know you as her Gardener. My spirit aches with such a longing for you to do a miraculous work in my sister's life today by colliding what she knows about you with what she believes about you. I'm asking today be a day of study that you remove anything that hinders her from seeing you clearly and then renew and restore her mind as you secure her up in the truth of who you are for her!

I've spent most of my Christian life living and feeding off what I knew about God, which isn't wrong because, after all, he is truth so you can't go wrong with that! However, what I did come to find, is when met with hardship, what I knew was exactly what came into question, revealing that something was disconnected in my belief system about God. I knew God was good, but I didn't believe it personally. I knew God was sovereign, but I began to wonder if that sovereignty was more like "ruling with an iron fist" instead of a loving hand. I knew God was kind, but he didn't feel kind to me. I knew a lot about God, but when the plane crash happened, much of what I knew, I realized I didn't believe. As Christians, what we know about God must collide with what we believe.

We are going to start building on the foundation laid yesterday by focusing our attention on the Gardener, God. I like to think of today as the day you take what we know about God and collide it with what you believe about God to produce the raw condition of your heart. This, dear one, is where authenticity is found in your relationship with God.

Please glance back at our Vine and Branches diagram as a quick refresher of John 15.

Now let's go and meet the Gardener in John 15:1. **Write the verse below**.

Before we move any further, **use the space below to write down what it is you believe about God**.

> *For this exercise, do not get hung up on whether it's right or wrong. If it's a characteristic you believe of him, it must be acknowledged. Authenticity happens when what we know and what we believe collide, so be authentic (not for his sake but for yours, because after all, he already knows your heart. It's we who are blind to our true heart condition).*

Now, let's look up each Scripture reference below and record what each verse says about God's goodness.

- Romans 8:28

- Isaiah 61:1 – 11

- 1 Peter 2:9

- Philippians 4:19

- 2 Corinthians 9:8

- Jeremiah 29:11

This is where I wish you and I were sitting in my living room with tea or coffee and having a dialogue about this. In a world gone numb to truth, I love and crave hearing what Scripture says because it's truth we can actually hold with our hands, but with that comes the diversity of our stories. I wish we could sit and talk about how we understand these verses to be true for our lives or maybe it's a lack of belief. Either way, there is something refining about conversations like these and I wish I could just sit and listen to you share these words you are writing down.

To end today, I'm asking that you embark on a journey through Scripture to hunt down more truth about God. I'm leaving you with a blank sheet of paper to fill up. Go hunt down truth, girlfriend!

> *Please do not skip this exercise or go on to Day 3 until this exercise is completed.*

The second half of this exercise: be honest with God about what you believe about these truths. You don't have to write anything other than the truths, but allow your heart to be honest every time you write a truth down as if to ask yourself, "Do I really believe this is true?"

Day 3

Is God Really Good

*

Today's Focus: *"But what about you?" he asked. "Who do you say I am?"*
(Luke 9:20 NIV)

We are going to add some miles to our journey by taking a detour from John 15 and heading over to Luke 9. Luke 9 reveals that people are starting to talk about and form ideas and beliefs about Jesus. It was around this same time he performed a miracle where he fed five thousand people with only five loaves of bread and two fish, which was a significant miracle to say the least! I can only imagine what the word on the street was about Jesus.

Take time to read Luke 9:18 – 20. Jesus asked his disciples about what others are saying about him. Why do you think he does this?

It seems to me Jesus wanted to know less of what the crowd was saying about him and more of what the disciples thought regardless of what others were saying. Jesus cared that the disciples had the right thinking of who he was, and he cares that we do too. It matters that both our knowledge and our beliefs about God line up to his truth.

Today, we begin to merge our knowledge of God with our beliefs of God, so it would be wise to pause here and **ask yourself, "What is it I believe about God as my Gardener?"**

After you have spent time here, take hold of the verses from yesterday (listed below) and **ask God to reveal your true beliefs about each promise for you personally.**

Directions for Merging Truth with Beliefs Exercise: Below you will see the verses you will use. Each verse holds a particular truth about God. **You will insert your name in the space provided after each verse**. This will be your entry into a dialogue with your Gardener about your belief about him as it relates to that particular truth stated in that Scripture. This is your space to confess and repent and boldly ask for right and complete thinking about who he is to you. If you find you are having a hard time believing anything these verses state, ask him to help you overcome your unbelief (Mark 9:24 NIV).

Merging Truth with Beliefs Exercise:

• Romans 8:28

_____, do you believe Romans 8:28 is true for you?

Why?

How has this impacted your life (your belief or lack of belief)

• Isaiah 61:1 – 11

_____, do you believe Isaiah 61:1 – 11 is true for you?

Why?

How has this impacted your life (your belief or lack of belief)?

• 1 Peter 2:9

_____, do you believe 1 Peter 2:9 is true for you?

Why?

How has this impacted your life (your belief or lack of belief)?

• Philippians 4:19

_____, do you believe Philippians 4:19 is true for you?

Why?

How has this impacted your life (your belief or lack of belief)?

• 2 Corinthians 9:8

_____, do you believe 2 Corinthians 9:8 is true for you?

Why?

How has this impacted your life (your belief or lack of belief)?

• Jeremiah 29:11

_____, do you believe Jeremiah 29:11 is true for you?

Why?

How has this impacted your life (your belief or lack of belief)?

There are going to be seasons and times in our life when we have a hard time lining up what we believe with what we know about God. Life is hard, and there is a real enemy that has come to kill, steal, and destroy (John 10:10). This exercise isn't about those seasons of life but your overall belief about God. You may be tempted to view this exercise as a list of "things to fix" but resist doing that because it's a complete waste of time if we are trying to be the fix-er and perfecter of our faith- that role is God's alone. We can trust that he will complete and perfect our faith. And remember, you are being tended to by the perfect Gardener, and this particular gardener always takes care of his Vine, to which you are connected (John 15).

Use today's exercise as a tool to pray over each of your responses to these verses. Then, ask God to heal and perfect the places of your heart that are broken so you can see clearly and trust fully that he is good to you.

Truth for Your Soul: *Being confident of this, that he who began a good work in you will carry it on to completion until the day of Christ Jesus (Philippians 1:6) and Looking unto Jesus the author and finisher of our faith.* (Hebrews 12:2a NIV)

Tomorrow we shift our gaze to the relationship between the Vine and Gardener. Before we enter that relationship, take one last time to ponder things between you and the Gardener by reading John 15:1 – 17 and soak in these past two days with him. Remember, we started today's journey by way of Luke 9, who do you say God is?

Day 4

Is God Really Good

*

Today's Focus: *I am the true vine, and my Father is the gardener. He cuts off every branch in me that bears no fruit, while every branch that does bear fruit he prunes so that it will be even more fruitful… This is to my Father's glory, that you bear much fruit, showing yourselves to be my disciples.* (John 15:1 – 2, 8 NIV)

Today we are settling our gaze on the true Vine who is Jesus. Jesus uses this particular parable to help his disciples understand the vitality of abiding in Jesus at all times, but this parable wasn't just meant for his disciples then but for all believers today. At some point in our faith, our basic knowledge of this passage must move us to a belief that abiding is necessary for living a full life in Jesus. If we don't know how to abide on the Vine at all times, in all seasons, we are like a wave of the sea, blown and tossed by the wind (James 1:6 NIV).

For your first activity for today, do a basic Google search for a picture(s) of grape vines. No-

tice how the fruit looks when growing. Consider the characteristics of the fruit.

What catches my eye almost immediately is how fresh and ripe the fruit looks. In fact, I don't notice any dead fruit on the vine, do you? For this to be true, can you imagine how closely the gardener must be tending to this vine? In order to keep it looking healthy, he is keeping a close eye on it, pruning what is dead, and then feeding and nurturing what is alive so it can produce even more fruit.

Now that you briefly put yourself in the shoes of a gardener, read John 15:1 – 17. Pray that these words would fall fresh on you as you read this chapter again. Eventually, these words will be so fresh on your mind that you can't get them out of your head, like a song that gets stuck in your mind and all you can do is sing it all day.

Here in this passage, you are witnessing the relationship of God and his Son. God takes care of his Son by keeping watch of his production of fruit. In turn, Jesus lives in perfect unity with his Father by submitting to the pruning of and producing of fruit. Let's put this unity between Father and Son under a microscope, and like a scientist to get a closer look and better understand.

Write out the verse to each Scripture reference below and record what you observe the Scrip-

tures to say about Jesus' unity and relation to his Father.

• John 5:19

• John 6:38

• John 10:30

• John 14:10

• John 15:10

• John 16:28

- These verses share about the unity of your Gardener and Vine.

Based on the above Scripture, how does Jesus' relationship with the Father directly impact believers? Seek out more Scripture to accompany your answer.

If you are a Christian, your life is impacted by your Vine and vice versa. But not only that, the Vine is impacted by the Gardener, and the Gardener by the Vine. Are you starting to see how all of this is working together for good? It was right here, at this point of study, that I had this awakening happen in my spirit that God really does work all things out for the good of those who love him. It was here where I ran to grab my notebook and started drawing out this scene as if I found a map leading to buried treasure!

This, dear one, is my prayer for you, that you have just as much (if not more) fresh revelation for yourself. I long for you to know him like this, as good. I long for you to feel something about his goodness that you can't contain it and must share it with others.

I've spent so many years of my life "knowing" but not really knowing his goodness. Could it be possible that we know, in our heads, God is good but don't really live like it because the truth is, we don't believe it in our hearts. **Will you take a rest on your journey and begin to record what the unity between the Vine and the Gardener means to you? How is your life impacted by their unity?** Until tomorrow…

Your Writing Space:

Day 5

Is God Really Good

*

Today's Focus: *Yes, I am the vine; you are the branches. Those who remain in me, and I in them, will produce much fruit. For apart from me you can do nothing.* (John 15:5 NIV)

Referring to our Scripture focus for today, the branches represent Christians. Our role, as a branch, is to abide on the vine. **I'd like you to think of someone in your life that has, from your lens, done this. Next, draw a picture of a branch below and label it with the name of that person.**

We are going to get really familiar with what Jesus says about the branches over the next couple of days because, after all, this deals directly with us! **Read John 15:1 – 17 and below write out any characteristics you read about that describe the branches.**

Next, write John 15:4 below.

We must abide in Jesus to produce any living fruit and to be fruitful. I think of all the times in my life I have worked tirelessly to be successful, the best at something, better than someone when really all I am called to do is abide in Jesus.

Let's kick up a little more creativity on today's journey by doing a simple google search on a picture of "vine and branches". Once you've found a picture of a vine that has an abundant amount of healthy fruit on it, consider what this fruit may look like if severed from the vine. **Let's record our thoughts by answering to the questions below.**

- What colors might you be seeing if this fruit was severed from the vine?

- Where might the fruit be located if severed from the vine?

- What other descriptive words can you think of to describe the difference of fruit on a branch verse severed from the vine?

When you are ready, I'd like to take a quick detour with you and give some biblical theology to help you digest what is true and refuse to translate anything untrue.

Truth for Your Soul: *You have already been pruned and purified by the message I have given you.* (John 15:3 NIV)

As we read these words in John 15, it's important to remember the narrative as a whole because things can get real wonky in our interpretation of Scripture as we pick apart and highlight a few verses at a time. With that in mind, I want to take some time to sit down together and do just that.

One important detail to note is seen in John 15:3 where Jesus is talking to the disciples. Here the disciples represent the branches which are attached to the vine. Therefore, we can know this is not a passage on salvation because the disciples are already saved. Instead, this passage is meant to be used as insight for a belief on producing fruit and abiding in Jesus.

There seems to be different interpretations of verse 6, and I want to make you aware of three of them. The purpose is because I don't want you to get confused on details or miss the main focus of this passage which is on believers. Below are these three different interpretations from a well-authored commentary:

> *These words have been interpreted in at least three ways: (1) the "burned" branches are Christians who have lost their salvation. (But this contradicts many passages, e.g., 3:16,36; 5:24; 10:28-29; Rom. 8:1.) (2) the 'burned' branches represent Christians who will lose rewards but not salvation at the judgment seat of Christ (1 Cor. 3:15). (But Jesus spoke here of dead branches; such a branch "is thrown away and withers.") (3) the "burned" branches refer to professing Christians who, like Judas, are not genuinely saved and therefore are judged. Like a dead branch, a person without Christ is spiritually dead and therefore will be punished in eternal fire* (Holman, John 2000).

Tomorrow we are going to discuss, in greater detail, the fruit bearing of a believer as discussed in this passage. Before we walk over that direction, I'd like to end by highlighting the three privileges of a believer. This is your heritage and right. May you walk fully in it through the rest of your journey, fellow sojourner.

1. Abide on the true Vine
2. Bear much fruit
3. Bring your Father great glory

Oh, Goodness the Bible Study

Week Four

Reflecting on God's to You

Day 1

Abide

*

Today's Focus: *When you produce much fruit, you are my true disciples. This brings great glory to my Father.* (John 15:7 NIV)

Last week we took one day at a time to soak in some truths of the Gardener and the true Vine. In addition, we started to unlock the key role of a branch, which we are going to expand on today. I hope you took time to ponder all last week in your heart because this is where a truly authentic relationship with Christ begins. It is in this place where knowledge pierces the heart and you can't ever be the same again; a life changed.

Please read John 15:1 – 17 and allow your ears to perk up when you read the word "fruit." **In your own words, summarize John 15:4 below.**

In order to produce fruit, we must remain in Jesus. Does your summary of verse 4 sound similar? Remember, abiding in Jesus is simply remaining in Jesus just as the branches remain on the vine as seen in John 15.

Truth for Your Soul: *whoever says he abides in him ought to walk in the same way in which he walked.* (1 John 2:6 NIV)

Let's go a step further by taking this personal by sharing honestly below.

• Write about a time you were adamant about abiding in Christ even though others didn't understand. If you can't think of a time for you personally, write about a time you witnessed someone else abiding.

- Abiding in Christ impacts a person's life. What impact did this experience have on your life?

There are going to be naysayers who do not understand or appreciate your role as a branch abiding on the Vine. Whether or not these people validate our choice to abide, should not dictate our response. Abiding in Christ isn't always going to feel good or gain social satisfaction, so we better get some guts about us and know what it is we are committed to doing: abide or abandon. Jesus has been everything to me, so in spite of all my flakiness and hypocrisy, I'm staying by the power of the Spirit. But that's just me and it may not be you. I wonder if you've ever asked yourself,

- Am I willing to abide on the true Vine?
- Do I even believe he is the true Vine?
- What other "vines" have I been trying to produce lasting fruit from? Is it working?

Maybe you aren't convinced that Jesus really is the only way to find soul satisfaction. Been there, lived that one too. The thing is, I've spent enough time there to know it doesn't hold true for long… maybe for a while but it didn't do me good for the long haul. In fact, it left wreckage on my life. Praise God for his redemption or else I don't know where I'd be today.

The truth is simple but is often made so complicated: anything other than the true Vine cannot produce lasting fruit. **Do you really believe that? Where is your soul most satisfied today? Challenge your thinking by asking yourself, "How are you sure this way of satisfaction is going to produce lasting fruit?"**

We must ask ourselves these questions and be able to give an answer if we have any intention of staying connected to the true Vine. We better know why we believe what we believe and think what we think because there is a deceiver out there and he's looking to tear you right off your Vine.

Truth for Your Soul: *The thief comes only to steal and kill and destroy; I have come that they may have life, and have it to the full.* (John 10:10)

Abide

It is important to me that you do not miss the key role of a branch. I've spent much of my life in bondage because I was trying to be the good girl, be the most successful, praying "x" amount a day. Simply put, I was storing up all the good I did and holding stock in it, in me. The truth is (and I hope you hear me here because there is so much love that comes with what I'm about to say) the only one we can hold stock in is Jesus. Prone to wander and not believe this truth, I've lived many years trying to earn my fruit. The truth is fruit isn't earned, it's entrusted. We earned all we can earn the day Jesus died and so our response must be to abide. We have been entrusted with this fruit because we remain on the Vine.

In order for you to filter all of this through Scripture and then take what the Lord has for you, we are going to stop here for today. He wants you to abide because it's good for you and honors his Father. He wants you to abide because he loves you.

Below, I'm listing some writing prompts that you are free to use in your alone time with him. End today knowing that you can be confident that he will finish the good work he started in you, even if you think you've royally screwed up what has become of your life (Philippians 1:6). We abide, he produces. **But before we just settle our minds on this as true, let's make sure it's piercing our hearts by considering the following questions with our Father:**

- You may know what it means to abide, but how does it look in your life?
- Dig into Scripture and find two or three promises of Jesus. How are you abiding in these promises?
- What may be holding you back from abiding in Christ?
- Can you abide in Christ in some areas but not all areas of your life?

Your Writing Space:

Day 2

Abide

*

Today's Focus: *But the fruit of the Spirit is love, joy, peace, patience, kindness, goodness, faithfulness, gentleness, self-control; against such things there is no law.* (Galatians 5:22–23 NIV)

We are really starting to pick up some traction as we focus in on God's goodness. **Let's keep that going by reading Galatians 5:22 – 23.**
We've spent time in John 15, enough at this point to be familiar with Jesus talking to his disciples about bearing much fruit that is lasting fruit. Is anyone else, other than me, curious about what everlasting fruit really is? I have read John 15 so many times over the course of my life, and it wasn't until age 30 that I finally asked the question to something I always just accepted… "What is lasting fruit anyway?"

I have spent so much time and energy on being hurt and frustrated with God over outcomes in my life that have been painful, and I'm not talking about petty things here. It wasn't until I made the choice to really be honest before him, specifically about how I felt about what his word said was true, that I started to uncover a broken belief system. I wanted God's goodness to always feel good, not just be good for me eternally. I wanted God's goodness to mean happiness, not joy among sorrow. I wanted God's goodness to look pain free, not doing a good work in me through the pain. I wanted blessings to mean an abundance of things and a carefree life. Everything I wanted was not what God had for me or intended me to have, so I was faced with a hard question… "Then is this (following Jesus) worth it?"

I didn't know and I didn't pretend to know. I was over the pretending and talking the Christian talk (without any real belief about it all). I knew this had to mean something to me or I'd be only fooling myself once again. It was in my uncertainty that God led me on a journey where he continued to pursue me, and I continued to pursue him through His Word. We began to embark on this journey together and one stop was Galatians 5.

Join me there by reading Galatians 5:22 – 23. After you have read these verses, highlight, in your bible, each Fruit of the Spirit and then write John 15 next to verses 22 and 23.

If you aren't one to highlight in your Bible then just highlight each fruit in your mind.

What you are encountering in Galatians 5 is the lasting fruit that John 15 talks about! If you are like me and wondered what is good, the fruit of the Spirit is a great place to start for context.

Now, as if you were looking at a cute outfit on a mannequin at Target (because who doesn't love Target?!), think about how you feel being clothed in these? How do these make you look? Was this really what you were expecting when you decided to follow Jesus? Are you excited about trying these on, or do you think you'd rather pass on to something else or just keep your old clothes because, after all, they are more comfortable...

We have got to know how we really feel about this being the lasting fruit Jesus wants us to bear. We must face our feelings of disappointment to excitement, discouragement to encouragement, or else we will remain uncomfortable, unsure, frustrated, and just possibly in our old rags of bondage (for sake of comfort). If we don't know how we feel about this and then take those feelings captive with Scripture, we will be controlled by our feelings which are often fickle and untrustworthy.

As you prepare to embark on your own journey, I'd like to leave you with some truth to help nourish you along the way. Think of this as your "care package."

It may not be nail polish or a magazine, but it will do you far better. It's time for you to "pack up" and head out alone with your Savior. Below is your care package of Scripture.

Care package:
Write out each verse below to be sure they are hidden in your heart in case there are any thieves along the rest of your journey.

• Philippians 1:6

• Romans 8:28

• Isaiah 61:7

• John 3:16

Day 3

Abide

*

Today's Focus: *I am the vine; you are the branches. If you remain in me and I in you, you will bear much fruit; apart from me you can do nothing.* (John 15:5 NIV)

Almost every night I sing, "Jesus Loves You," to each of my children. I sing it often because it's a truth I want tattooed on their minds as they grow. They may not always feel loved by Jesus in their life, and it's in those exact seasons I pray this truth with resurface for them. I don't know what they will experience in life, but I do know that their feelings will have them for good if they don't know how to line it up with truth. I know that they cannot allow their faith to be dictated by how they feel, or they will be weak-willed. I know that, in the seasons of deep pain, they must armor up with the words of God and not allow their feelings to dictate truth. I know because, at one time in my life, this was me—weak-willed and controlled by my feelings.

My bondage took me closer to the Enemy than I ever care to be again, and it was because I didn't know what to do with these feelings that so counter-acted with Scripture. But, I did know truth because my mom boldly told us about God's truth as early as I can remember. She wasn't one to sugar coat Scripture, if it was in the Bible, we were told about it plainly. Simply put, it was rare if we were ever told a Bible story children's style, if you catch my drift.

It makes me smile remembering her in this way. She had a fire burning so fiercely inside of her that she was serious about God's Word and telling it to her children. Quite frankly, this is one of the kindness acts my mom did for me as a kid, made truth so perfectly clear that I couldn't escape it even as I tried to deny it during my young adult years. A beautiful legacy left by a woman who so loved her Heavenly Father.

As we start today, I want you to fill in your name in the blanks below. Then, just as I do for my kids and my mom did for me, envision your Heavenly Father singing this over you. He loves you, dear one, and this truth is for you... just as you are.

Jesus loves me
This I know,
For the Bible tells me so;

Little ones to Him belong;
They are weak, but He is strong.

Yes, Jesus loves _____*!*

Yes, Jesus loves _____*!*

Yes, Jesus loves _____*!*

The Bible tells me so.

Let's join back up with John over in John 15 for a moment. **Write John 15:2 below:**

Because God loves you and he loves his son, he must prune you so that you can bear fruit and much of it. I wonder what your thoughts are on being pruned? Does this mean anything to you at all, or is this just a verse in John that you accept as reality for a believer? **I think it might be a good idea if you took a moment and jot down some of these thoughts that you have when you read John 15:2.** Allow your mind to meet your heart and find the words to write your true thoughts…

Definition of Prune: reduce the extent of something by removing superfluous or un-wanted parts, trim by cutting away dead or overgrown branches or stems, especially to increase fruitfulness and growth (Merriam-Webster, 2017).

Your Writing Space:

Truth for Your Soul: The pruning of God is kind.

The pruning is God's kindness, yet it can produce pain and sometimes severe pain. After all, it is a cutting off of something that is a part of us, even if that something is dead.

In fact, take a moment to imagine shears being taken to you as you are pruned. If we read John 15:2 and have some idealistic interpretation that "it's all going to work out" as if to mean the pain won't produce too much suffering, agony, discomfort, aching, irritation, or discomfort, then a season of pain may be the undoing of you.

Truth for Your Soul: *Then you will know the truth, and the truth will set you free.* (John 8:32 NIV)

The purpose of this next exercise is to prepare you for the pruning and help you see why it is good of God. Listed below are all the fruits of the Spirit from Galatians 5. **Your job is to write the antonym of each fruit of the Spirit.** You've got to know, the Enemy always works in opposition to God, so if God is wanting to produce lasting fruit, the Enemy wants you producing dead fruit. A part of your preparation in the pruning is knowing your opponent and what it is he wants you producing. I did the first one for you as an example.

Love - Hate

Joy

Peace

Patience

Kindness

Goodness

Faithfulness

Gentleness

Self-Control

If God enables us to produce the fruit of the Spirit, you better believe the Enemy is going to fight to get us producing the opposite. Anything opposing the fruit of the Spirit is dead and must be pruned. It sounds good and right, doesn't it? But what happens when it hurts, and the shears of pruning look a lot bigger and more painful than you thought? This is where Romans 8:28 comes into play.

As tomorrow's preparation, write Romans 8:28 below.

Pruning causes us to feel something, but it's that feeling that causes us to trust God and that is always for our good. I'd like to share with you a personal example, to better explain what I mean.

A Season of Pruning

My Personal Testimony

I've spent most of my life learning to live and thrive in fearful circumstances. Much of my circumstances growing up were out of my control, so, in my mind, I had two choices: learn to deal with it or have it deal with me. I thought I was choosing the "deal with it" road, so I was completely dumbfounded when I realized fear was actually dealing with me.

As I grew up, so did my fear. It grew into something bigger than I could control and it began controlling me. Fast-forward to the first tragedy I had to deal with as an adult, and that fear seemed to grind itself deeper into my heart and become me instead of just something I "threw on" every now and again like a sweater.

Let me tell you something about being in bondage to fear, it suffocates you until it nearly kills you. It's almost as if fear likes to torment its slaves by taking you as close to death as possible until it releases its grip to let you breathe again. You quickly learn not to take too many breaths because he'll pull the leash on you to remind you that you're still his slave.

Fear is not a fruit of the Spirit. In fact, it is the opposite of joy because it robs us of all joy. Fear was something in my life that had to be pruned off. But, it was gut-wrenchingly painful, and I never want to have to learn that way again.

My experience of having fear pruned off has been exponentially long and excruciatingly hard. I spent nearly six years in this constant state of pruning and it nearly slaughtered me. In fact, there were times I wished it would have just killed me because the pruning was that painful. You see, I was losing a part of myself... something I nurtured for years of my life: fear.

It was in the pain of the pruning that God resurfaced very specific truths to my mind, and although pained by the pruning, I couldn't escape these resurfaced truths. One of which was, "The thief comes only to steal and kill and destroy; I have come that they may have life, and have it to the full" (John 10:10 NIV).

This has to be him giving me new life, I'd thought. So, I held on a little longer until one day, I was free. And then, Maria's pruning of this deeply entangled dead fruit was starting to produce something worthwhile, something that will last me in times of great joy and pain.

Write Romans 6:11 below.

Although I am not absent of fear, I am most definitely not in bondage to it. This makes me think of the lyrics from the hymn "I Have Decided to Follow Jesus". Take a moment and soak in the lyrics below.

I have decided to follow Jesus;
I have decided to follow Jesus;
I have decided to follow Jesus;
No turning back, no turning back.

Though I may wonder, I still will follow;
Though I may wonder, I still will follow;
Though I may wonder, I still will follow;
No turning back, no turning back.

The world behind me, the cross before me;
The world behind me, the cross before me;
The world behind me, the cross before me;
No turning back, no turning back.

Though none go with me, still I will follow;
Though none go with me, still I will follow;
Though none go with me, still I will follow;
No turning back, no turning back.

Will you decide now to follow Jesus?
Will you decide now to follow Jesus?
Will you decide now to follow Jesus?
No turning back, no turning back.

Truth for Your Soul: *And we know that in all things God works for the good of those who love him, who have been called according to his purpose.* (Romans 8:28 NIV)

I'd like to end today by giving you some time to reflect and write about your own pruning. I've shared with you a part of my story, but all of this means nothing if we don't embark on your own journey. Pray and write, and I will see you tomorrow!

Day 4

Abide

*

Today's Focus: *And we know that in all things God works for the good of those who love him, who have been called according to his purpose.* (Romans 8:28 NIV)

Yesterday we talked about how the Lord prunes his people so they can produce more fruit for his glory. **Please circle the word "His" in the Romans 8:28 verse above.**

We learned that pruning is most often painful, and you took some time thinking about that yesterday as you imagined what it would be like to be pruned with shears.

It is not pessimistic to acknowledge that life is painful and will be painful. In fact, I'd like to suggest that we would be ill-equipped if we are unprepared for pain. In the chapter following John 15, Jesus says, "I have told you these things, so that in me you may have peace. In this world you will have trouble. But take heart! I have overcome the world" (John 16:33 NIV). I've spent many years writhing in fear all because my heart didn't accept that God's goodness may not always feel good. Below, I'm sharing one of my journal entries with you where I desperately tried to understand God's goodness in a time that was not good.

The Gardener and the Griever
from July 2012

I am scared because I don't see how this can be worked for my good. I am waiting for the next "pin to drop" and have no idea how to live life any other way than this because it's come to be my way of protection of my hurting heart. I try not to think of the pain, at least not the depth of the wounds their death has left.

I am scared to forget them: their laughs, smiles, how their hugs felt, their smell, how they looked at me, how Mom's hair laid, how holding her hand felt, how Dad always played with his hands when he talked. I don't want to forget even if it is painful.

Most days I feel numb. If I allow myself to really think on the depth of the loss, I think my heart will explode with pain. I can barely move, but I feel I could muster up just enough strength to run from all this pain that stands in front of me like a mountain I know I have to go over in order to get to the other side.

Oh Lord, I want to physically hurt so my heart and body could be on the same page. I want to tear my heart out, bruise and beat my body so they will see this is how it feels every second inside. Am I experiencing all of this in vain, Lord? How is this for my good, God? How can I ever be used if I can't even move?

I want security and goodness to feel good but that's never going to happen on this side of heaven, is it? I don't know how to find security in you knowing this. I want you, and yet, I'm just learning how little I even know you.

Father, I am begging you to show me how this was for my good, and if it wasn't... just show me that too, so I can stop being tortured by all of this. Help me understand your goodness in this.

Your Daughter,
Maria

Today I want to address a belief that many hold onto that is tied up with being pruned. Romans 8:28 says, "And we know that in all things God works for the good of those who love him, who have been called according to his purpose." **If you are following Jesus, please insert your name in the blank below.**

I, _____, know that in all things God works for my good because I have been called according to his purpose.

As you hold to Romans 8:28, open up to Psalm 136:1. **Please write this verse below.**

Based on the Scriptures in Romans and Psalm we can know that God is good and will work all things for our good. **Without restraint, share what these truths mean to you.**

This is where I wish we were sitting over coffee and talking face to face. I'd love nothing more than to hear the unrestrained version of your heart. The beauty is, God knows—and that's really all that matters.

So now I have to ask you, what if God's goodness doesn't always feel good? **Take some time to consider this question.**

Truth for Your Soul: *Search me, God, and know my heart; test me and know my anxious thoughts. See if there is any offensive way in me, and lead me in the way everlasting.* (Psalm 139:23–24 NIV)

A few years ago, I did some reflection of my own and I'm sharing this with you today. Below you will witness the woundings of a grieving daughter. God used this painful season to expose a heart of unbelief in his goodness. **It was in his kindness he revealed my true heart's condition so that I may experience a soul fully healed.**

Reflections of a Grieving Daughter
Summer 2011

Father, I'm so confused by words offered up to me by well-meaning people. Help me know what is true or just a version of truth. I know they intend for it to bring encouragement but why do I feel so discouraged, misunderstood, and insecure in my grieving as if I'm grieving wrong? Lord, am I grieving in a way that dishonors you? I don't know how else to grieve than to be honest ...

I've come to hate idealism. Every time I hear "everything happens for a reason," "I bet God is going to do something big through this," "God is going to use (insert person) in a big way," "they are finally home, we can rejoice in that" as if to say I'm not but Lord, can't I hurt too? I hear these words from the well-meaning and I cringe and cry.

Are these the words a grieving person has to receive and just take in the heat of their grief? Can't you see the pain my soul bears? Please shut the mouths of the well-meaning but ill-equipped. Save me from their words that cut my already wounded heart. Can I have a moment to breathe and be in pain before I'm told to rejoice? Am I missing something, Lord? Should this feel good to me that they are dead? "But they are more alive than they've ever been," the well-meaning say. I know this Lord; I don't doubt this for a second. It's just that… I'm not. I'm still here and this still hurts.

Should I be outwardly rejoicing their death? Isn't it possible to be pained and yet trust your goodness? Can pain and grief coexist? If it can't, Lord, I feel I can't survive this thing.

What if they are right, Lord? Maybe everything does happen for a reason, so if that's true, does that somehow mean their deaths had to happen for this (whatever "this" is) to happen? Did they have to die for you, God, to do "some big miracle?" Help me know what is true, what you define as good.

I need truth to sound above the noise of the well-meaning. I want to know truth. I need to know truth.

Your daughter is in pain,
Maria

Are you asking him to teach you truth? May I suggest that it isn't until you sit in the place of frustration with him alone, without the noise of others, that you will then discover and know—without a doubt—what is truth for your soul. I've spent nearly fifteen years allowing others to tell me what is true of God, but it wasn't until my thirtieth year of life—where he became my sole teacher—that I truly began to know truth and I'll never be the same again. This, dear one, is true life change and he is the only life changer. I wonder if we truly believe this?

You've spent time today pondering what God's goodness really means. Ladies, to be equipped to be mighty women of God, we have got to be cross-trained where we are culture-trained. Culture is training you to believe goodness is based on how you feel, but the cross is training you that our feelings do not have to dictate truth. Truth sets us free. Feelings can keep us in a state of constant confusion if never aligned with the Truth.

Truth for Your Soul: *Then you will know the truth, and the truth will set you free.* (John 8:32 NIV)

Take some time and reflect on today's study of God's goodness. When you are ready, **write Romans 8:28 in your own words below.**

Are you struggling because you desperately want God's goodness to always feel good?

I did too.

It feels like a crushing blow when this truth is met with your inescapable reality that life—no matter how many years pass, new life that grows, exciting experiences that arise—is now filtered through the lens of pain. But this is where hope comes in, dear one. We can look forward with the hope that someday God's goodness will always feel good because all will be made right (Revelation 21 NIV). As you wait expectantly for that day, you can experience healing of the most broken place right now: your soul.

I'm so grateful for the testimony of Katherine and Jay Wolf in their book Hope Heals,

> *No amount of catharsis or perspective finding will change the fact that our situation is terribly sad and deeply broken. I can give God the glory, and it can still hurt. I used to cry myself to sleep*

every night. But I have learned, above all other lessons, that healing for each person is spiritual. We will be fully restored in heaven, but we are actually healed on earth right now. My experience has caused me to redefine healing and to discover a hope that heals the most broken places: our souls (p. 18).

Knowing what you believe about God's goodness is a big deal in your relationship with him. **Spend time in his Word and prayer today, asking him to reveal his goodness to you.** Sending you off with this encouragement: it's his kindness that leads us to repentance (Romans 2:4 NIV)! You do not stand condemned by him: not now, not ever! So, whatever you are believing about his goodness—or lack thereof—confess it to him and then ask for his help to walk in complete repentance. Like Peter, run to Him.

Day 5

Abide

*

Today's Focus: *I no longer call you servants, because a servant does not know his master's business. Instead, I have called you friends, for everything that I learned from my Father I have made known to you.* (John 15:15 NIV)

I have been anxiously awaiting today because we are going to be bringing it all together. I hope this merging of truth has already been happening for you as you've opened and completed each day's study. Today we are focusing in on Jesus' friendship with you and your history with him. To kick us off, please read and record John 15:14–16 below.

Based on Scripture you just read, fill in the blanks below by inserting your name.

If you, _____, do what he commands,
               then Jesus calls you,

_____, his friend.

These verses hold some beautiful and rich truth that we cannot simply gloss over.

You have got to know that the only other known reference of being called a friend of Jesus is with Abraham in James 2:23 (Holman). It is so tender and kind of God to reserve these words for you. Let that sink into your heart for a moment before you read on.

The beauty of this intimacy does not rob Jesus of his sovereignty as Savior of our souls and here's why,

> *We need to remember, particularly in this day of easy language about relationships with God, that the friendship of this passage is not reciprocal. Jesus may call the disciples his friends, but they still address him as Lord and Master. In fact, that is the pattern of the entire Bible* (Holman, John 15:15).

I don't want you to miss that, although Jesus calls us his friends, he will always be looked on as our Lord, Savior, Master, Redeemer, Restorer. I would have done you a great disservice if you left today's study with the mindset that you and Jesus are buddies. **Please fill in the blanks below, starting by writing your name.**

Jesus calls me, _____, friend yet I call him _____.

> * Fill in the last blank with a truth about who Jesus is in Scripture. Think about who he is to you: Master, Teacher, Healer, Redeemer, Restorer...

Truth for Your Soul: *For he has clothed me with garments of salvation and arrayed me in a robe of his righteousness... For as the soil makes the sprout come up and a garden causes seeds to grow, so the Sovereign Lord will make righteousness and praise spring up before all nations.* (Isaiah 61:10–11 NIV)

With the proper view of what friendship with Jesus means, **please reread John 15:15–16 and record what this means to you below.**

I'd like to travel all the way back to Week Two, Day Four for the remainder of our time today. On that day, you spent some time reflecting on your life and God's faithfulness during specific seasons of your life. Feel free to take some time and look back at that day's journey as a reminder.

By now we have some more history documented for you to work with—that has been recorded over the weeks spent in this study. You will use that history recorded to go back and add to your timeline. Below are some helpful instructions to get you started.

Helpful Tips for this Exercise:

My hope is that you take time to really sit and pray about this final exercise. I greatly desire for there to be an opening of your eyes and heart to ways he has been faithful that you haven't yet seen. **Think back on times you've been disappointed, hurt, fearful and ask God to help you identify how he has been faithful through those times. Think back on times you've been overjoyed, excited, content and ask God to help you identify how he has been faithful through those times.**

I implore you to ask him for eyes that see past the surface response and straight to the intimate ways he has pursued you through his faithfulness. You may even find it helpful to think back on Galatians 5, the Fruit of the Spirit, and recognize how you can testify to the production of this fruit in your life.

Finally, record all these new reminders of his faithfulness on your timeline from Week Two, Day Four. I encourage you to keep this timeline as your evidence that your God is good and faithful to you! I hope you find yourself adding to it throughout the rest of your journey here on this earth.

I must leave you here so you can go and meet up with your Savior and embark with him only. He has stories of his faithfulness to remind you of. I pray that you enjoy him. He so enjoys you.

Life is not always going to be easy, but remember that we've wised up about God's goodness in the heat of pain. We know that his goodness isn't dictated by how we feel but by the truth of His Words!

Below is a truth for you to take along for the remainder of your journey ahead. Hide this in your heart and guard it with everything you have, for there is still a thief on the loose … for now.

Truth for Your Soul: *being confident of this, that he who began a good work in you will carry it on to completion until the day of Christ Jesus.* (Philippians 1:6 NIV)

The writing of this study has been so tender to me that I can't imagine my heart ever leaving the hands of the woman who picks this up to complete. I am praying for you as you continue to embark on this journey of knowing and resting in God's goodness. I desire nothing more than for you to be free from your unbelief and trust the goodness of God in your life. I can say with all sincerity, I know you can be free and walk mightily in assurance that God is good to you and for you.

Embarking,

Maria Bowersock

P.S. I'm inviting you to go further by completing the epilogue assignment. I hope you find encouragement there!

Epilogue Assignment
The Good Shepherd
How to Recognize His Voice

*

We spent the last four weeks embarking on a journey that led us down a road of personal discovery of God's goodness. We can close the last week of study knowing the perfect Gardener works all things out for the good of the Christ follower, the fruit bearing branch, because we are connected to his true Vine. Simply put, God can't be anything but good. He just doesn't have it in him to be kind of or somewhat good.

It would only be appropriate as we depart, we take one more good look at our Savior's goodness from the vantage point of the Good Shepherd in John 10. This will be our final farewell of walking this road together.

There is something so human about Jesus in this scene that I don't want you to miss. Instead of writhing in his hurt and pain of others or using it as a teaching opportunity on forgiveness, he used this time to remind that he is the Good Shepherd who leads and cares for his sheep. After much time discussing him as the true Vine, this is a perfect place to settle in before we part ways. I leave you in the hands of the Good Shepherd.

Day 1
The Good Shepherd
How to Recognize His Voice

*

Meet me over in John 10. How appropriate that we
are concluding our study of God's goodness by
looking at the Good Shepherd. **Please record verses
1 – 5 below.** It's a beautiful thing to see the very
words of God written in our own handwriting.

**Reflect on ways you see the tender care of the
shepherd in these verses. Record anything that is
meaningful to you.** For deeper study: after you have
read it through once and recorded, go back and read
through it again. This time, ask him to help your
eyes see more ways he cares for you that are meaningful. John 15 says we can ask for anything in his
name, so let's get to asking!

Today I leave you with a challenge to prepare you for your journey alone with your Father. Do you know your Father's voice? If not, how are you going to get to knowing it and why do you want to? May I suggest that it's not until we know the answers to the "how" and "why" questions that we will do it without later abandonment.

Day 2
The Good Shepherd
How to Recognize His Voice

*

I am so thankful Jesus shoots straight with us, so we don't wander off into the slaughtering of our souls without knowing better. It is in his kindness that he makes truth so perfectly clear. **Please write out verses 6 – 10 below.**

Over the course of five weeks we have talked about God's goodness from the vantage point of John 15 and John 10; producing much fruit on the true Vine and being taken care of by the Good Shepherd. The reality is, unless we are true Christ followers, we will not experience God's goodness in its purest, most protective form. Verse 9 talks about salvation, and, quite frankly, our lives depend on it, so let's make sure we have a clear understanding of how Scripture defines salvation. **Based on John 10:9, how is a person saved? Record your answer and any other Scripture that comes to your mind below.**

Reading truth and knowing truth are both good and necessary. However, it's not until we take these words personally that a fire is lit under our feet to do something with them. **So, with that in mind, what about you? Have you "come in through Jesus?" Share below.**

His purpose is to give you a rich and satisfying life in him. Is this what you are experiencing? If not, why do you think that is? May I be so bold to suggest that it's not until we believe something is true that we actually decide to do it. So, I have to ask, do you believe Jesus truly is rich and satisfying?

Day 3
The Good Shepherd
How to Recognize His Voice

*

Thank you, Father, for knowing those who are yours. I am so relieved to know I can be fully known by someone, and that someone being the Good Shepherd. **For the sake of committing this to memory, write out verses 11 – 15 below.**

These verses tell a beautiful story of Jesus as our good shepherd in that he didn't come just to protect us from our predators but to intentionally die for us, his sheep. This makes him a shepherd unlike any shepherd ever known to man.

As you think on this, what do you want to say to your Good Shepherd? **Record the words kept in your heart below.**

Day 4
The Good Shepherd
How to Recognize His Voice

*

The Good Shepherd holds all authority, yet tenderly cares for and leads his sheep. **Record verses 16 – 18 below.**

How does Jesus' authority over death yet his role as our Good Shepherd impact your life?

Conclude today by reading Isaiah 40:11 and record his tenderness shown for you in this verse below. My purest hope is for you to begin to see his tenderness toward you personally because it is a wildly beautiful revelation that leaves you changed.

Day 5
The Good Shepherd
How to Recognize His Voice

*

It appears that the more Jesus described Himself as good and true, the angrier the Jews became. **Please write out verses 19 – 21 below.**

I have to ask, how do you respond the more Jesus reveals himself to you? Some respond in fear and worry about "what if." Others respond in confidence and certainty of "even if." How we respond to Jesus speaks volumes of who our hope is in, which directly impacts how we view God: as good or not. We must be willing to face this question with authenticity and audacity to be as such.

I've cherished this time with you, fellow sojourner. My deepest hope is that you now have the tools to discover God's goodness in your own life. This is your freedom! I pray you will continue to embark on this journey of discovering God through the faithful words of Scripture. He never promised it would be easy, but he did promise that it will be worked for our good. Through the blood and blisters, remember that it is producing what only he can: something good (Galatians 5:22 – 23).

To Him who completes the good work He started, farewell.

Forever Embarking,
Maria Bowersock

Endnotes

Bible Translations Used
The Bible. English Standard Version, Crossway, 2001.
The Bible. New International Version, Zondervan, 2000.

<u>Week 2</u>
page 30
"Sift | Definition of Sift in English by Oxford Dictionaries." *Oxford Dictionaries | English*, Oxford Dictionaries, 2019, en.oxforddictionaries.com/definition/sift.
an online dictionary with multiple editors

page 34
Hitchcock, Roswell D. Hitchcock's New and Complete Analysis of the Holy Bible. New York: A.J. Johnson, 1871. Database, 2005 WORD*search* Corp. found in the section "Hitchcock's Dictionary of Bible Names"

<u>Week 3</u>
Page 78
Gangel, Kenneth. *Holman New Testament Commentary - John.* Nashville, Tennessee, Broadman &

Holman Publishers, 2000. Database, 2005 WORD-*search* Corp.

Week 4
page 97
Wolf, Katherine and Jay. *Hope Heals*. Grand Rapid, MI, Zondervan, 2016. page 18.

Made in the USA
Monee, IL
11 November 2019